Published by Smart Apple Media,
an imprint of Black Rabbit Books
P.O. Box 3263, Mankato, Minnesota 56002
www.blackrabbitbooks.com

Published by arrangement with
The Salariya Book Company Ltd

Cataloging-in-Publication Data is available
from the Library of Congress

Printed in the United States
At Corporate Graphics,
North Mankato, Minnesota

9 8 7 6 5 4 3 2 1

ISBN: 978-1-62588-339-1

Illustrator: Nicholas Hewetson

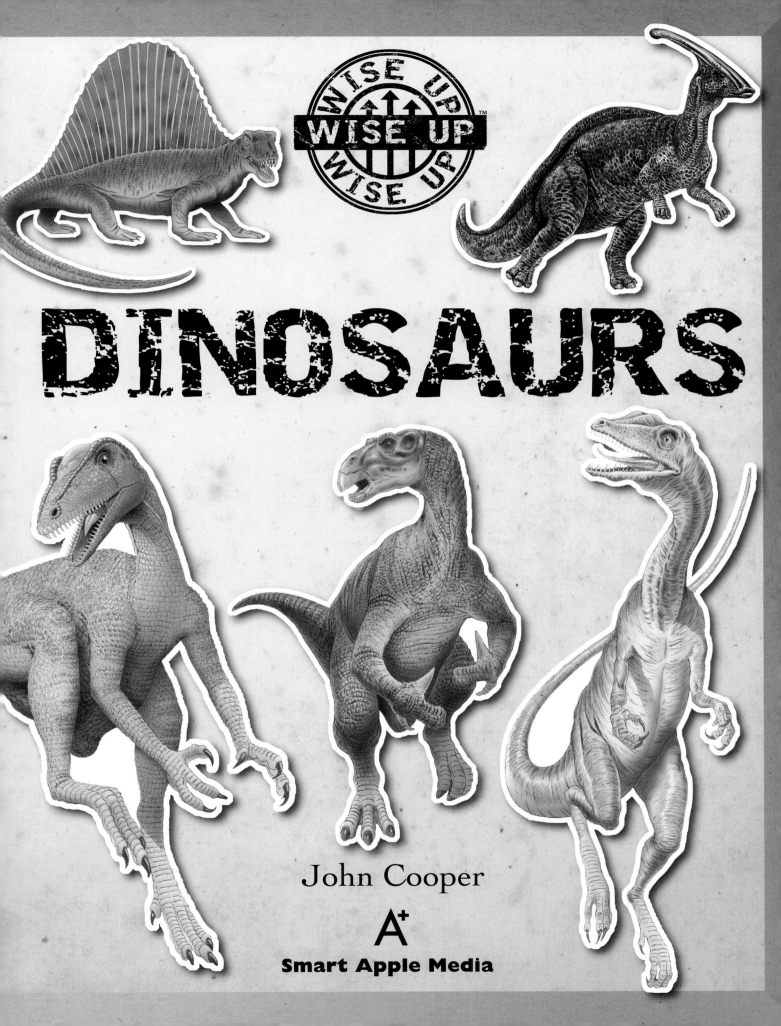

DINOSAURS

John Cooper

A+

Smart Apple Media

Contents

The Age of Dinosaurs

inosaurs were animals that lived during the Mesozoic era of Earth's history—from 250 to 65 million years ago. They were reptiles, a group of animals which today includes lizards, snakes, and crocodiles.

Timeline

▶ **The Cretaceous Period** 145–65 million years ago. The continents started to form the shapes we recognize today. The South Atlantic opened up and was soon followed by the North Atlantic.

▶ **The Jurassic Period** 205–145 million years ago. The continents were splitting and seas divided the land.

▶ **The Triassic Period** 250–205 million years ago. All the continents were joined together in a single supercontinent. Inland, the climate was very dry.

◀ Modern fish, flowering plants, and birds evolved. The climate cooled.

◀ Many of the largest dinosaurs evolved.

◀ Start of the Jurassic Period.

◀ Dinosaurs were widespread across the supercontinent.

◀ The world's earliest known dinosaur, *Eoraptor*, evolved in Argentina 225 million years ago.

◀ Start of the Triassic period.

Dinosaurs were not the first reptiles. The remains of the earliest known reptile were found in Scotland in 1989; it lived about 335 million years ago. Dinosaurs were suited to a land-based life because their legs, held under their bodies like our own, were good for carrying weight, for hunting, and for running.

▲ A monitor lizard's legs splay out at either side of the body. The weight of the animal is carried by the joints.

Diplodocus lived between 150 and 140 million years ago and was 88 feet (27 m) from head to tail.

▲ Crocodiles and some other reptiles improved their strength and speed by having legs partly tucked under the body.

A *Pteranodon*'s wing span was over 16 feet (5 m). It lived 85–64 million years ago.

A pigeon's wing span is almost 1 foot (30 cm).

Deinonychus existed 110–100 million years ago and was about 10 feet (3 m) long.

Stegosaurus dinosaurs lived about 150–140 million years ago and were about 24 feet (7 m) long.

Modern crocodiles are about 12 feet (3.5 m) long.

There are a few familiar extinct reptiles that were not dinosaurs. Pterosaurs flew, while ichthyosaurs and plesiosaurs lived in the sea.

◀ Dinosaurs like *Triceratops* had their legs positioned directly under the body for strength and agility, just like birds and mammals today.

Dinosaur Ancestors

Somewhere in South America, about 250 million years ago, the first dinosaurs appeared—reptiles capable of racing swiftly on upright legs and capturing prey with their specialized jaws and teeth. Such early fossils have not been found, but evidence of their descendants, living only 25 million years later, has been discovered. An almost complete skeleton of the world's oldest known dinosaur, named *Eoraptor*, was found in Argentina in 1991.

FACTFILE
DIMETRODON
Group: Reptile: Pelycosaur
Size: Almost 10 feet (3 m) long
Diet: Small reptiles
Where: North America
When: 80 million years ago

◀ This sail-backed early reptile had the sprawled legs typical of slow-moving reptiles. *Dimetrodon*'s sail contained blood vessels which could heat up quickly to spur the reptile into action, or help to cool it down when overheated.

▲ *Longisquama* was a lizard-like creature from Asia that lived 240 million years ago. Long, stiff scales covered its body and back. Its wing-like structures may mean it could glide.

▼ Scientists had long believed that the first dinosaurs were small, meat-eating hunters—exactly what *Eoraptor* proved to be. This fierce hunter was about 3 feet (1 m) long.

Eoraptor

▼ The sleek and slender *Lagosuchus* had legs like a dinosaur's and could run quickly to catch its prey. Some scientists think that it was the ancestor of all dinosaurs. Its legs are typical of running animals. The shin bones are almost twice the length of the thigh bones.

Lagosuchus

FACTFILE
LAGOSUCHUS

Group: Reptile: Thecodontian
Size: About 1 foot (30 cm) long
Diet: Grubs, insects
Where: South America
When: 250 million years ago

FACTFILE
EORAPTOR

Group: Dinosaur: Theropod
Size: About 3 feet (1 m) long
Diet: Small reptiles
Where: South America
When: 225 million years ago

Early Dinosaurs

The earliest dinosaurs entered the hot, barren world of the Triassic period, around 250 to 205 million years ago. Lush vegetation existed only near coasts and rivers. While plants provided food for many small creatures—insects, grubs, lizards, amphibians, and mollusks—they in turn became food for the new and aggressive meat-eating dinosaurs. These first carnivorous dinosaurs remained small but they were still at the top of the food chain. There is evidence, too, of dinosaur cannibalism!

▶ Wide-eyed and nimble, *Procompsognathus* must have been more than a match for any small animal in the deserts of Europe in late Triassic times.

FACTFILE
PROCOMPSOGNATHUS

Group: Dinosaur: Theropod
Size: Almost 4 feet (1.2 m) long
Diet: Small reptiles, mammals, and insects
Where: Germany
When: 215 million years ago

Herrerasaurus

FACTFILE
HERRERASAURUS

Group: Dinosaur: Theropod
Size: Almost 10 feet (3 m) long
Diet: Reptiles and small mammals
Where: Argentina
When: 225 million years ago

▶ *Compsognathus*, one of the smallest known dinosaurs, stood no taller than a chicken, but was a hunter, built for speed.

◀ Fragments of *Saltopus*, a small reptile unearthed in Scotland, appear to be from a cat-sized creature with long legs and short hands. It may not even be a dinosaur.

▶ *Staurikosaurus*, found in Argentina, was the oldest known dinosaur until *Eoraptor* was unearthed. It was a fast and dangerous hunter.

◀ *Coelophysis* skeletons found in New Mexico have hollow bones. *Coelophysis* was a strong and swift hunter. Two skeletons contained bones of smaller *Coelophysis*—devoured youngsters. This dinosaur was a cannibal!

▶ *Herrerasaurus* was much bigger than its cousin *Eoraptor* and may have hunted it when other prey was scarce. Its large head and sharp teeth made it a dangerous enemy.

FACTFILE
LILIENSTERNUS
Group: Dinosaur: Theropod
Size: Over 16 feet (5 m) long
Diet: Larger reptiles
Where: Germany and New Mexico
When: 220 million years ago

▼ Found in Europe and the U.S.A., this large hunter was equipped with slashing claws on hands and feet. Fossil skulls show that *Liliensternus* may have had a bony crest, like the later carnivore, *Dilophosaurus*.

Dinosaur Vegetarians

Plant-eating (herbivorous) dinosaurs became common in the Triassic world soon after the first carnivores. Once established, they spread quickly. Fossils of these "prosauropods"—early plant-eating dinosaurs—have been found in rocks between 230 and 178 million years old and from every continent, including Antarctica. They soon grew to a large size and were the ancestors of even bigger, long-necked sauropods such as *Apatosaurus*.

◀ *Yunnanosaurus* could feed on low vegetation and overhead leaves. Its long neck helped it reach foliage left by short-necked herbivores. Its chisel-like teeth easily shredded tough leaves.

FACTFILE

YUNNANOSAURUS

Group: Dinosaur: Prosauropod
Size: About 23 feet (7 m) long
Diet: Plants
Where: Southern China
When: 210 million years ago

FACTFILE

LESOTHOSAURUS

Group: Dinosaur: Ornithischia
Size: Over 3 feet (1 m) long
Diet: Ground-covering plants
Where: Lesotho, southern Africa
When: 190 million years ago

▶A quick runner, *Lesothosaurus* used speed to escape from carnivorous dinosaurs.

▼ *Pisanosaurus*, about 3 feet (1 m) long, was one of the very first herbivorous dinosaurs. It is known only from a single fragmented skull and skeleton found in Argentina.

◄ *Plateosaurus*'s jaws contained dozens of small, leaf-shaped teeth ideal for shredding food, but not for chewing.

Plateosaurus

▲ *Plateosaurus* had a defensive thumb claw to make up for its lack of speed.

FACTFILE

PLATEOSAURUS

Group: Dinosaur: Prosauropod
Size: About 23 feet (7 m) long
Diet: Plants
Where: England, France, Germany, Switzerland
When: 210 million years ago

► Like all herbivorous dinosaurs, *Lufengosaurus* probably had stones (gastroliths) in its stomach to help grind tough plant food into a more digestible form.

FACTFILE

LUFENGOSAURUS

Group: Dinosaur: Prosauropod
Size: About 20 feet (6 m) long
Diet: Plants
Where: Southern China
When: 200 million years ago

In the Jurassic period, Earth's continents split apart and the climate became cooler and wetter. Plants, especially ferns and conifers, became widespread, providing much better food for herbivorous dinosaurs. New dinosaurs thrived on this banquet and the long-necked, long-tailed sauropods soon became the largest animals ever to walk on land. Such huge dinosaurs had to consume massive amounts of food. Their increased size meant that walking on four feet became necessary.

FACTFILE

BRACHIOSAURUS

Group: Dinosaur: Sauropod
Size: About 75 feet (23 m) long
About 39 feet (12 m) high
Diet: Tree leaves and shoots
Where: Tanzania, East Africa;
Algeria, North Africa;
western U.S.A.
When: 152–145 million years ago

▲ With its long neck and strong jaws, *Brachiosaurus* was superbly equipped to feed on overhead trees.

▲ The neck of *Mamenchisaurus* was quite stiff and probably could not be lifted to a great height. It perhaps fed on low-lying vegetation, grazing as it swept its head from side to side.

FACTFILE

MAMENCHISAURUS

Group: Dinosaur: Sauropod
Size: Over 72 feet (22 m) long
About 16 feet (5 m) high
Diet: Plants
Where: Sichuan, China
When: 145 million years ago

▼ Enormous hip and back bones were discovered in New Mexico in 1979. The back vertebrae above the hips were fused together to form an immensely strong beam which bridged the hind legs.

▶ The skull of *Seismosaurus* was probably rather small.

FACTFILE
SEISMOSAURUS

Group: Dinosaur: Sauropod
Size: 125–170 feet (38–52 m) long
            About 12 feet (3.5 m) high
Diet: Plants
Where: Western U.S.A.
When: 120 million years ago

▲ A sauropod's shoulders and back form an arch. Mounted on four pillar-like legs, the structure is very strong.

◀ A sauropod's slim build would be an advantage when walking in heavily wooded areas.

▼ *Seismosaurus* swallowed stones which helped to grind down rough plant food. More than 240 of these gastroliths were found when skeletons were first excavated. The largest was about 4 inches (10 cm) across.

◥ The necks of sauropods contained 12 to 15 vertebrae (*Mamenchisaurus* had as many as 19). Their necks combined minimum weight with maximum strength.

▼ *Seismosaurus* and other sauropods had feet like an elephant's, with five short toes on each foot.

Ferocious Dinosaurs

No dinosaurs have captured the imagination as much as the huge meat-eaters. The fierce but small hunters of the Triassic period evolved into the terrifying killing machines that preyed on the grazing herbivores of the Jurassic and Cretaceous periods. Armed with ferocious teeth set in enormous, powerful jaws, they could overcome just about any other animal. Only the largest sauropods may have escaped being their prey.

Tyrannosaurus

FACTFILE
TYRANNOSAURUS

Group: Dinosaur: Carnosaur
Size: Over 42 feet (13 m) long
Diet: Reptiles, dead or alive
Where: North America, China, Mongolia
When: 70–65 million years ago

▲ *Tyrannosaurus rex* is perhaps the most famous of all dinosaurs. It was also one of the last. Scientists still puzzle over the value of its tiny arms, which didn't even reach its mouth!

▲ Found in the deserts of the Sahara, the mighty *Carcharodontosaurus* puts even *Tyrannosaurus* in the shade.

▼ The enormous skull of *Carcharodontosaurus* is over 5 feet (1.6 m) long. The teeth are similar to those of the giant white shark, and the name means "shark-toothed reptile."

▲ The scale of a human skull shows the enormous size of this dinosaur.

FACTFILE
CARCHARODONTOSAURUS

Group: Dinosaur: Carnosaur
Size: Over 39 feet (12 m) long
Diet: Reptiles
Where: Morocco, North Africa
When: 90 million years ago

▼ *Tyrannosaurus rex* chases the sauropod *Alamosaurus* into a lake.

◄ Some scientists believe that *T. rex* was a fast runner and a deadly hunter, as shown here. Others think that it was a slow runner that fed on dead or dying animals, rather like a vulture.

Grazing herbivorous dinosaurs would constantly look out for carnivores. Like zebras or gazelles today, many prey species would graze in herds for safety. The sheer size of gentle giants like *Mamenchisaurus* might put off an attack from even the largest *Tyrannosaurus*. Others evolved defensive weapons and armor plating to provide protection from physical attack. A wide variety of horns and spikes, clubbed tails, and claws have been found as fossils. Rival male dinosaurs probably also fought for the leadership of herds and for supremacy in mating.

▲ *Styracosaurus* lived about 80 million years ago in North America. The frill of the largest male would have frightened off rivals, while its single horn was a deadly weapon.

FACTFILE

TRICERATOPS

Group: Dinosaur: Ceratopsia
Size: 30 feet (9 m) long
Diet: Plants
Where: North America
When: 70–65 million years ago

▼ Each of *Triceratops*'s three massive horns was covered with a tough, sharp sheath made of a similar substance to human fingernails. They were very impressive weapons. Its neck was well protected by a solid bony frill.

▲ *Centrosaurus*'s central horn was surrounded by a frill edged with bony knobs.

Triceratops

▶ More than 50 skulls of the herbivorous *Triceratops* have been found. They can measure up to 4 feet (1.2 m) long.

▲ With three horns and a large frill, *Chasmosaurus* was well prepared! As with many other horned dinosaurs, the frill was not solid bone but had openings covered only by skin.

▲ Scientists think that *Anchiceratops* and many other horned dinosaurs fed in herds. Under attack, all the adults could stand side by side to form a fierce wall of horns and frills.

◀ Armored dinosaurs such as *Euoplocephalus* had unique methods of defense. The skull and the body were protected by a shield of bony plates, short spines, and spikes.

▶ The heavy lump of bone on the end of the tail could deliver a massive whack!

FACTFILE

STEGOSAURUS

Group: Dinosaur: Stegosaurid
Size: Over 24 feet (7.5 m) long
Diet: Plants
Where: North America
When: 140 million years ago

▶ The bony plates of *Stegosaurus* looked alarming, but their function was probably to allow the dinosaur to warm up and cool down more efficiently.

▶ The bony spikes at the end of the tail were highly dangerous.

Most types of dinosaur are believed to have laid eggs with hard shells, like birds' eggs. Egg remains have been found all over the world, most famously on "Egg Mountain" in Montana and in the Gobi Desert of Mongolia. Identifying which dinosaur laid which egg is difficult, unless skeletons of young dinosaurs are found nearby. Rarely, eggs are discovered in which the bones of the embryo dinosaur still exist. We know that some dinosaurs made nests. A clutch of 24 eggs laid by the small carnivore *Troodon* was found in Montana, surrounded by a protective rim of mud. A skeleton of *Oviraptor* was found in Mongolia, still sitting on its eggs!

▲ Large groups of *Maiasaura*, an herbivorous dinosaur, laid eggs in colonies of nests between 90 and 65 million years ago.

▲ Each nest was positioned so that a parent guarding one nest could not interfere with any other chick or parent. The nest was made out of soil and vegetation.

Maiasaura eggs were laid in batches. Each egg was about 5 inches (12 cm) long and roughly spherical. Despite their enormous size, dinosaurs did not lay enormous eggs. The shells had to be thin enough for the chicks to break out, and to allow oxygen to pass through.

▶ *Maiasaura* probably brought food to the nests, just as parent birds do for chicks today.

Maiasaura

The first *Oviraptor* skeleton was found lying on a nest of eggs thought to be from a *Protoceratops* dinosaur. *Oviraptor* means "egg thief," and with its toothless beak it was thought to live mostly on eggs. More finds of *Oviraptor* with eggs have been made since. Recently, one of these eggs was discovered to have an *Oviraptor* inside, not a *Protoceratops*. So *Oviraptor* is no longer labeled a thief.

Oviraptor

▶ Long, narrow eggs were typical of *Oviraptor* and some other types of dinosaur. Usually, more than 20 eggs were laid at a time. Each egg was about 6 inches (15 cm) long. Most eggs have no fossilized contents, because many embryos died before their bones had hardened.

Tracking Dinosaurs

Footprints left by a herd of *Brachiosaurus* in the muddy shores of a lake in Texas are still around 80 million years later. Dinosaur footprints give us clues which are impossible to discover from fossil bones, teeth, or eggs. They can tell us a lot about the daily activities of dinosaurs. Fossil footprints come in all shapes and sizes, from chicken-sized prints to enormous sauropod prints, three times larger than those of elephants. They have been found on all continents except Antarctica. Some footprints are found just a few at a time, others in their millions across vast areas of land.

▲ Carnivorous theropod dinosaurs like *Allosaurus* were bipedal (two-footed). Their feet were equipped with sharp claws, useful weapons for capturing and killing prey. Theropods usually walked "pigeon-toed," placing one foot in front of the other.

▲ *Corythosaurus* was one of the hadrosaurs or "duck-billed" dinosaurs. As with many bipedal herbivorous dinosaurs, each foot had three toes and, instead of claws, each toe ended in a blunt sort of hoof. Such feet were useful equipment for escaping from predators!

▲ The feet of sauropods like *Apatosaurus* had to carry their enormous weight. Each foot was a large, rounded pad with the toes splayed out to help spread the load. The inner toe of each foot carried an especially long claw, useful for self-defense or for gripping branches.

▲ The distance between footprints can be measured to calculate speed. *Albertosaurus* may have run as fast as 28 m.p.h. (45 k.p.h.).

◥ *Iguanodon* probably walked on its hind legs most of the time, but fed on all fours to reach low-lying plants. Its large hind feet made big three-toed prints and its forefeet made smaller, horseshoe-shaped prints. Its left footprint is clearly different from its right footprint.

◀ Aprons worn when performing the Hopi Indian Snake Dance include dinosaur footprints in the design, showing that dinosaur tracks were discovered by North American Indians long before scientists.

▶ Deep theropod footprints in Colorado provide natural paddling pools. This small boy gives a useful idea of scale.

▼ *Iguanodon*'s chest contains an unusual bone which may have helped strengthen it, assisting the dinosaur to walk on all fours.

▶ The *Iguanodon*'s "thumb" was a sharp spike which could not touch the other fingers, but stuck out. It was almost certainly a defensive weapon which could be used to slash at attacking carnivores.

Iguanodon

▶ With short front legs and long hind legs, *Iguanodon* was in danger of falling forward when on all fours. To prevent this, it had a thick, muscular tail which had stiffening rods of bony tendons running along it. This balanced the dinosaur from the hips.

FACTFILE

IGUANODON

Group: Dinosaur: Ornithopoda
Size: Over 29 feet (9 m) long
Diet: Plants
Where: Europe, North America, Mongolia
When: 120–110 million years ago

▶ The middle three fingers of each forefoot are nearly joined and slightly spread out. If the *Iguanodon* used its hands for walking, they may have been covered with a tough pad of skin.

The Last of the Dinosaurs

The last of the three geological periods in which dinosaurs lived was the Cretaceous period, when Earth's climate was warmer than now. About half of all known dinosaurs lived at that time. Other forms of life—mammals, snakes, birds, insects, flowering plants, and broadleaved trees—flourished then, too. But the global temperature began to fall. This affected all the plants and animals living at the time. There were fewer large sauropods, the horned dinosaurs and the duck-billed hadrosaurs became more common, and the "thick-headed" dinosaurs evolved. *Tyrannosaurus rex* and its cousins ruled the carnivores.

▲ During the Cretaceous period, from 145 to 65 million years ago, Earth's single huge landmass changed. The continents drifted apart and were divided by large seas. This affected the climate.

FACTFILE
Parasaurolophus

Group: Dinosaur: Hadrosaur
Size: Almost 33 feet (10 m) long
Diet: Plants
Where: Western North America
When: 80–65 million years ago

▶ Along the old Cretaceous shores of the western U.S.A. and Canada, masses of hadrosaur bones have been found. Large numbers of dinosaurs seem to have died together, perhaps because of a flood. But why such large groups? Perhaps the hadrosaurs had learned to migrate, to move south for the winter to find more supplies of food.

Parasaurolophus

▼ Several types of "duck-billed" dinosaurs had strange bony crests on their skulls. They contained hollow bony passages which were joined to the nostrils. It seems likely that these crests were used like the tubes of a trumpet and could produce loud honking noises for display or threat.

The first bird we know of was *Archaeopteryx*, which lived 150 million years ago. Many scientists now believe that birds evolved from small carnivorous dinosaurs. By the end of the Cretaceous period, most of the modern groups of birds had appeared. *Presbyornis* was an early duck-like bird from Europe, the U.S.A., and South America. *Ichthyornis*, from the U.S.A., had teeth in its beak and probably fed on fish.

▼ Many types of "thick-headed" dinosaurs evolved, not only in North America but also in Mongolia, Europe, and China. *Pachycephalosaurus* was the largest. The thickened skulls were probably used for fighting between competing dinosaurs.

FACTFILE

PACHYCEPHALOSAURUS

Group: Dinosaur: Ornithischia
Size: Over 26 feet (8 m) long
Diet: Various plants
Where: Western North America
When: 70–65 million years ago

◥ The skulls of dinosaurs like *Pachycephalosaurus* had up to 9 inches (23 cm) of bone on top.

26

The End of the Dinosaurs

Under the Caribbean Sea, off the northern tip of the Yucatán Peninsula in Mexico, there is a circular crater 110 miles (177 km) wide. This is the best evidence yet of a gigantic explosion—the impact of a comet about 9 miles (15 km) wide hitting Earth about 65 million years ago. Did this comet cause the dinosaurs to disappear? Well, maybe, but other things were happening on Earth at the same time. Seas had invaded the land everywhere, so there were fewer dinosaur habitats. In India and Pakistan, huge volcanoes pumping out masses of lava significantly affected the climate. Perhaps all three causes combined to bring about the end of the dinosaurs, and possibly half of all known backboned animals.

▼ The impact of a comet would have thrown enormous quantities of rock and dust into the atmosphere, blocking out the sun globally. Plants withered and died, so herbivorous dinosaurs went hungry and died. Soon the carnivores, too, starved and died. Small creatures might hibernate, or survive on grubs and roots. When the sun finally reappeared, seeds germinated and life carried on—but without the dinosaurs.

▼ The last vertebra is positioned, then the skull is added.

▼ Dinosaur skeletons in museum displays are not made of the original fossils, because they are too valuable to use. Replica bones, made out of fiberglass or resin, are lighter and can be displayed with minimal support. However, making a replica dinosaur skeleton is hugely expensive and a very skilled job.

Dinosaur hunting entails finding rocks of the right age to contain fossils: rocks laid down during the dinosaur era. They must also be the right type, deposited in layers by rivers or lakes, in deserts or near swamps and lagoons. Fossil hunters search on cliffs and in quarries, high up on mountains, or in hot, barren places. An experienced eye can search for clues that dinosaurs were in the area, such as fossils of the plants that the dinosaurs fed on, or shellfish and fish fossils from the lakes where they gathered to drink. With luck, a bone will be seen sticking out from a layer of rock, and maybe the rest of the skeleton lies beneath. Then the hard work really begins.

▲ A fossilized bone is found, and exposed by scraping away the surrounding rocks. Photographs and drawings are made.

▲ As the bone dries in the air it may need to be painted with resin to protect the fragile and cracked surface.

▲ Rock is slowly cleared away from each side of the bone until it is supported only by a narrow pillar of rock underneath.

▲ The bone is covered in wet tissue and strips of plaster bandage. This hardens and protects the exposed fossil.

▲ The bone, sealed in plaster, is removed from the ground. The underneath part is then covered in plaster, too.

▲ The bones are taken to a museum, where the plaster jackets are cut away to reveal the bones. Any remaining rock is removed and the bone is carefully cleaned.

▲ More delicate work is possible in a laboratory. The lighting is good, specialized tools are available, and the use of microscopes allows the finest of repairs.

▲ The scientists identify the bones, then work with artists to establish how the bones might fit together and what the dinosaur may have looked like when it was alive.

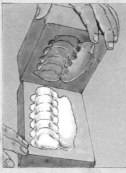

▲ The bones are used to produce molds in rubber to create replicas. The delicate originals are then handled less often and copies can be sent around the world for study.

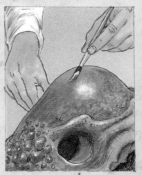

▲ The copies are carefully painted so that they exactly match the appearance of the original bones. Replicas are displayed so the originals can be kept in storage.

The neck vertebrae begin at the shoulders, starting with the largest of the neck bones.

The vertebrae from shoulder to hip are threaded onto a carefully bent rod of steel which is then fixed to two supports between the front and back legs.

The legs are also threaded onto steel supports which are then hung from the central rod together with the ribs.

The tail vertebrae are threaded onto the steel rod in order: largest first, smallest last.

Dinosaur Quiz

1. **What is the world's oldest known dinosaur called?**
   a) *Eoraptor*
   b) *Lagosuchus*
   c) *Dimetrodon*

2. **Which dinosaur seems to have been a cannibal?**
   a) *Herrerasaurus*
   b) *Compsognathus*
   c) *Coelophysis*

3. **Prosauropods were early types of which kind of dinosaur?**
   a) Herbivorous
   b) Carnivorous
   c) Armored

4. **Where was the dinosaur *Mamenchisaurus* found?**
   a) North America
   b) China
   c) South America

5. **Hundreds of dinosaur eggs have been found on "Egg Mountain." In which country is this?**
   a) Mongolia
   b) Canada
   c) United States of America

6. **What unusual weapon did *Iguanodon* have?**
   a) A tail spine
   b) A thumb spike
   c) A horn

7. **What may the long bony crest of *Parasaurolophus* have been used for?**
   a) Making mating calls or threatening noises
   b) As a defensive weapon
   c) As a snorkel

8. **Tri means "three." What did *Triceratops* have three of?**
   a) Toes on each foot
   b) Frills around its neck
   c) Horns on its head

9. **In which geological era of time did the dinosaurs live?**
   a) The Paleozoic era
   b) The Mesozoic era
   c) The Cenozoic era

10. **What is the oldest known fossil bird called?**
    a) *Archaeopteryx*
    b) *Presbyornis*
    c) *Protoceratops*

Quiz answers

1) a see pages 8–9
2) c see page 11
3) a see page 12
4) b see page 14
5) c see page 20
6) b see page 23
7) a see page 25
8) c see page 18
9) b see page 6
10) a see page 25

Glossary

ancestor An early form of an animal or plant from which later forms have developed.

bipedal Standing or walking on two legs.

carnivore Any animal that eats the flesh of other animals as its main food source.

carnosaurs A group of large carnivorous dinosaurs with huge skulls and enormous teeth, such as *Tyrannosaurus*.

Ceratopsia A group of dinosaurs that includes all the horned dinosaurs from the late Cretaceous period, such as *Triceratops*.

comet An object in the solar system that travels around the sun and is made of ice and rocks. The frozen material evaporates as it nears the sun and forms the comet's tail.

conifer A cone-bearing tree, usually evergreen, such as fir or pine.

Cretaceous The geological period that began about 145 million years ago and ended about 65 million years ago.

embryo The young of an animal developing within an egg or womb.

evolve To change gradually from one form to another.

fossil The remains of a plant or animal, buried in the ground and gradually turned to stone.

gastrolith A stone or pebble, swallowed by an animal and kept in its gut. Gastroliths help to grind up food which is difficult to digest.

hadrosaurs A group of large herbivorous dinosaurs that lived during the late Cretaceous period. Many had bony skull crests and duck-billed jaws.

herbivore Any animal that eats plant material as its major food source.

Jurassic period The geological time period that began about 205 million years ago and ended about 145 million years ago.

Mesozoic era A major division of geological time, 250 to 65 million years ago, which included the Triassic, Jurassic, and Cretaceous periods.

Ornithischia A group of herbivorous dinosaurs with a hip structure similar to that of birds.

Ornithopoda A group of ornithischian dinosaurs, such as *Iguanodon*, that generally walked on two legs and had three-toed feet.

pelycosaurs A group of early reptiles that developed about 300 million years ago. It is believed that they were the ancestors of mammals.

plesiosaurs A group of large swimming reptiles that lived in the seas and oceans during the Mesozoic era.

predator Any animal that hunts and then eats another animal.

prosauropods A group of dinosaurs that lived during the Triassic and Jurassic periods. They were among the first of the large herbivorous dinosaurs.

pterodactyl A short-tailed pterosaur that lived during the Jurassic and Cretaceous periods.

pterosaur A group of flying reptiles that first appeared during the Triassic period.

quadrupedal Standing or walking on all fours.

saurischians A group of dinosaurs with hip structures similar to those of lizards.

sauropods A group of very large, herbivorous, quadrupedal dinosaurs such as *Diplodocus* and *Mamenchisaurus*.

stegosaurids The group of dinosaurs which includes *Stegosaurus*, all of which have one or two rows of bony plates or spines along the back. They lived during the Cretaceous and Jurassic periods.

theropod A carnivorous, saurischian dinosaur such as *Compsognathus*.

Triassic period The geological time period that lasted from ca. 250 to ca. 205 million years ago.

vertebrae The bones that make up the neck, spine, and tail of all backboned animals.

Index